Whatever the drama,
the stars have the answer...

ASTROLOGY IRL

Straight-talking life advice
direct from the stars

POP PRESS

ASTROLOGY IRL

Straight-talking life advice
direct from the stars

CONTENTS

GOT DRAMA?

Then why not take some advice from the stars? Whether you're facing a big-ass life decision or just trying to nail the small stuff, let your horoscope give you a helping hand. From figuring out your dream job to planning a first date, as well as your perfect work out, how to win at Mondays, how to deal with your boss and where to go on holiday, the stars are ready and waiting with wisdom, insight and LOLs.

Are you in need of some tough love, or someone who'll give it to you straight and help you make sense of the madness? Or perhaps you'd like to feel inspired to try something new? Or maybe you just want to know what your crush is really thinking . . . Housemates, career, exercise, self-care, house parties or date night – whatever the drama, dip into *Astrology IRL* and let the stars help you take care of it.

HOW TO USE THIS BOOK

Just as the sun is the brightest, most vital object in the sky, your sun sign is the part of your astrological chart that other people can see shine from you. This is the big picture stuff, at the centre of who you are. It's what we mean when we say 'What's your sign?' If you don't know yours (or want to find out someone else's), turn over the page . . .

The changeover dates from one sign to the next are sometimes different from year to year. So if your birthday is on the cusp of two signs, you might want to check it online against your birth year, in case it's different to the one that's shown here (it's all to do with that sneaky extra quarter of a day we get each year, which is also the reason we have leap years). You can do this and find out more at www.francescaoddie.com/freecharts.

Even though your sun sign (AKA your star sign) is generally seen as being at the cornerstone of your horoscope, there's other stuff going on that influences how you respond to life, how you feel about things, and how others see you. Apart from your sun sign, the two biggies are your rising sign and your moon sign. If you want to know more about how your moon sign affects your inner, private self and your rising sign determines how you project your personality out into the universe, turn to the back of this book. Some people feel like there's at least one characteristic of their sign that doesn't really resonate – if this is you then your natal chart (a highly individual map of the skies at the exact moment you were born) will most likely show a load of planets in another zodiac sign, which will shed light on this difference. We hope you have fun reading the wisdom of the stars in these pages, and are inspired to find out even more about the mysteries of the heavens when you're done ...

SCORPIO

ARIE

LIBRA

TAURUS

GEMINI

PISCES

CANCER

SAGITTARIUS

THE SIGNS

CAPRICORN

VIRGO

o

AQUARIUS

THE SIGNS IN THREE

And their cosmic catchphrases . . .

ARIES
21 March – 19 April
Enthusiastic, Impatient, Pioneering
'Go hard or go home'

TAURUS
20 April – 20 May
Calm, Determined, Possessive
'All in good time'

GEMINI
21 May – 20 June
Adaptable, Restless, Networker
'If you don't like it, change it'

CANCER
21 June – 22 July
Sensitive, Defensive, Funny
'Nourish to flourish'

LEO
23 July – 22 August
Magnanimous, Generous, Proud
'Be a unicorn in a field of horses'

VIRGO
23 August – 22 September
Observant, Humble, Critical
'The devil is in the detail'

LIBRA
23 September – 22 October
Courteous, Charming, Superficial
'Style is always in fashion'

SCORPIO
23 October - 21 November
Passionate, Intense, Controlling
'Never apologise, never explain'

SAGITTARIUS
22 November – 21 December
Enterprising, Adventurous, Undisciplined
'Buy the ticket, take the ride'

CAPRICORN
22 December – 20 January
Responsible, Dignified, Sober
'You can't always get what you want'

AQUARIUS
21 January – 19 February
Impartial, Tactless, Unconventional
'Try everything once'

PISCES
20 February – 20 March
Compassionate, Kind, Disillusioned
'Life is a mystery'

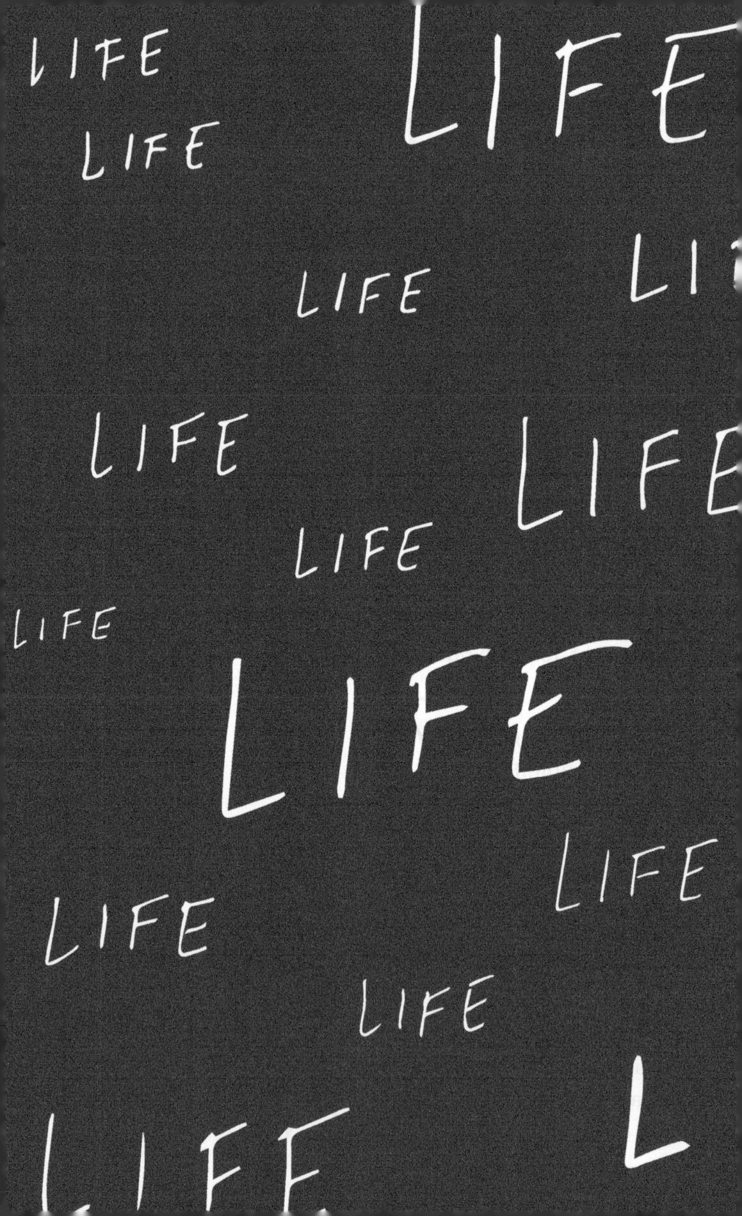

LIFE
LIFE
LIFE
LI
LIFE
LIFE
LIFE
LIFE
LIFE
LIFE
LIFE
LIFE
LIFE
L

LIFE
LIFE
LIFE
LIFE
LIFE
LIFE

YOU GOT THIS

LIFE
LIFE
LIFE
LIFE
LIFE
LIFE
LIFE
LIFE
LIFE

HOW TO SUPERCHARGE YOUR MORNING

Whether you're an early riser, or a duvet hog . . .

Up and at 'em

ARIES Minimalism is life: shower and get out.

VIRGO Embrace the routine. Get up at the same time every day.

LEO Pre-plan your outfit, and put on some great tunes.

LIBRA Schedule a full hour to preen and get your outfit on point.

SAGITTARIUS Fling open the windows and drink in the possibility of the day!

CAPRICORN Get to the office before everyone else.

Hitting the snooze button

TAURUS Set three alarms. Put one in the kitchen.

GEMINI Get connected: check the news, WhatsApp your gang.

CANCER Make breakfast for your housemates – feeding your gang will get you out of bed.

SCORPIO Focus on your tasks and avoid people.

AQUARIUS Don't hang around, grab a coffee, listen to a podcast.

PISCES Pull a tarot card for the day and set a mantra.

WORK OUT YOUR WORK OUT

Exercise to suit your sign

CANCER, LEO, VIRGO

Aerobics, CrossFit, weights – feel the burn, get the bod.

ARIES, SCORPIO, CAPRICORN

Running, swimming, cycling – unleash your competitive spirit, work out to win.

GEMINI, LIBRA, AQUARIUS

Netball, football, running club – knowing your gang is waiting for you will get you out of bed.

TAURUS, SAGITTARIUS, PISCES

Yoga, hiking, wild swimming – connect to more than a treadmill.

PERFECT BRUNCH

ARIES Somewhere they take bookings.

TAURUS Where the portions are big and beautiful.

GEMINI That place your friend went last weekend, it looked great.

CANCER At home, brunch is your speciality.

LEO A party brunch that rolls into an all-dayer.

VIRGO Somewhere that caters to your latest health fad.

LIBRA Only there to take photos, someone else can choose.

SCORPIO Somewhere dark and intimate.

SAGITTARIUS Must be bottomless.

CAPRICORN Set menu.

AQUARIUS Anywhere with communal tables so you can chat to strangers.

PISCES Anywhere that serves mimosas.

TIME KEEPING

Do you keep everyone waiting?

TAURUS, CANCER, SCORPIO
Half an hour early.

VIRGO, ARIES, CAPRICORN
Bang on time.

AQUARIUS, GEMINI, LIBRA
Five minutes late.

SAGITTARIUS, LEO
Half an hour late.

PISCES
Oh sorry, was that today?

CAFFEINE FIX

What's your sign's order?

ARIES Espresso.

TAURUS Green tea.

GEMINI Frappuccino.

CANCER Builder's tea.

LEO Espresso macchiato.

VIRGO Decaf coffee.

LIBRA Oat milk caffè latte.

SCORPIO Double espresso.

SAGITTARIUS Hot chocolate.

CAPRICORN Cappuccino.

AQUARIUS Turmeric latte.

PISCES Irish coffee.

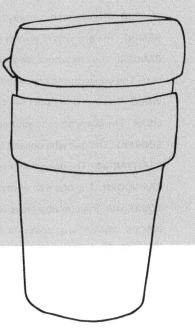

HOUSEMATE HOROSCOPE

What kind of roommate will they be?

ARIES The one who is up and out at 7am.

TAURUS The one who is always in their PJs by 7pm.

GEMINI The one who is always on their phone.

CANCER The one whose ice cream you steal.

LEO The one with the best wardrobe.

VIRGO The one who tidies the cupboards.

LIBRA The one who asks your opinion on their outfits.

SCORPIO The one who doesn't leave their room.

SAGITTARIUS The one who leaves mess everywhere.

CAPRICORN The one who always buys the loo roll.

AQUARIUS The one who plays computer games till 3am.

PISCES The one who cooks for everyone but forgets to turn the oven off.

HOSTING

When you invite the signs round for dinner, they . . .

ARIES Stay til 1am, even though they're running a half-marathon the next day.

TAURUS Will come if they rate your cooking.

GEMINI Will come if they rate the other guests.

CANCER Totally honestly? Would prefer to stay home.

LEO Will make an effort and turn up looking great.

VIRGO Offer to bring their own food if the menu isn't gluten free.

LIBRA Try to take control of dessert.

SCORPIO Will talk intensely with one person all night.

SAGITTARIUS Want to know if everyone is going dancing after.

CAPRICORN Drive over to avoid drinking.

AQUARIUS Are distracted by their phone all night.

PISCES Offer to pick up the wine.

WHERE ARE MY KEYS?

ARIES Pocket.

TAURUS On the counter at your favourite coffee shop.

GEMINI Check all your bags.

CANCER Kitchen table.

LEO Last night's jacket.

VIRGO On the special hook, of course!

LIBRA Who had them last?

SCORPIO At your one night stand's house.

SAGITTARIUS THEY COULD BE ANYWHERE.

CAPRICORN Desk at work.

AQUARIUS In the fridge.

PISCES Still in the front door.

PERFECT PETS

Which animal suits your star?

ARIES Dragon.

TAURUS Tortoise, the ultimate gentle friend.

GEMINI Rat, clever and surprising like you.

CANCER Guard dog.

LEO Sponsor a tiger.

VIRGO A collection of low-maintenance succulents.

LIBRA Siamese cat.

SCORPIO Snake.

SAGITTARIUS A few dogs, a cat and a horse … maybe a goat.

CAPRICORN Hamster (you relate to the wheel).

AQUARIUS An exotic bird.

PISCES The ugliest pet in the animal shelter.

I'LL BE THERE FOR YOU

Who should you turn to in a crisis?

CANCER, PISCES

For hugs and unlimited sympathy.

VIRGO, SCORPIO, CAPRICORN

To come up with an action plan and make damn sure you stick to it.

GEMINI, PISCES

To confess your sins, with no judgement.

TAURUS, LIBRA

To calm you down.

ARIES, GEMINI, LEO, LIBRA, SAGITTARIUS

To take you out on the town and drown your sorrows.

SCORPIO, SAGITTARIUS, CAPRICORN, AQUARIUS

To tell it how it is, even if you don't want to hear it.

COULD YOU BE BETTER AT SAYING SORRY?

Resist your default . . .

ARIES Look, I said I'm sorry.

TAURUS Sorry.

GEMINI OMG, I'm so sorry, I promise it will never happen again!

CANCER *Crying* I only did it because you made me feel so sad!

LEO Buys you a gift.

VIRGO Writes you a note.

LIBRA Apologises quickly, changes the subject.

SCORPIO Would rather die than apologise.

SAGITTARIUS *Shocked* Sorry! I had no idea!

CAPRICORN After a long brooding silence and depression, says sorry.

AQUARIUS It's history. Stop being upset about the past.

PISCES *Can't stop crying*

TOUGH CALLS

What to do when you can't decide . . .

ARIES Taking quick decisions is your superpower!

TAURUS Sleep on it.

GEMINI Call everyone you know.

CANCER Discuss it with the family at dinner.

LEO Trust your instinct.

VIRGO List the pros and cons.

LIBRA Ask your best friend, debate at length.

SCORPIO Keep your options open.

SAGITTARIUS Toss a coin.

CAPRICORN Take your time.

AQUARIUS Call a friend.

PISCES Wait for the answer to arrive in a dream.

<u>WHAT YOU WANT VS WHAT YOU NEED</u>

	What you want	Try
ARIES	To win and be the best.	Asking friends or colleagues for advice about a problem and taking it.
TAURUS	Nothing to ever change.	Hot desking for a week, you can do it.
GEMINI	To know everything about everyone.	A week without gossip.
CANCER	Family time.	Planning a trip to somewhere you've never been.
LEO	To be appreciated.	Taking a friend out for lunch and finding out how they really are.
VIRGO	Control and order.	A whole day where you let other people make the decisions (without interfering!).

	What you want	Try
LIBRA	To be loved by everyone.	Being more direct. Don't just pull the strings, come out and say it.
SCORPIO	No one to find out your secrets.	Telling someone you love about something that's been bothering you.
SAGITTARIUS	To travel the whole world.	Spending an evening making your home feel more cosy and beautiful.
CAPRICORN	To take over the world.	Taking a moment at the end of the day to reflect on what went well.
AQUARIUS	Equality for all.	Organising a get-together and focusing on connecting with your closest friends.
PISCES	To heal the world.	Doing a self-care MOT. What will make you feel better in the long run?

SPIRIT ANIMAL

ARIES Wolf. Independent and slightly dangerous.

TAURUS Sloth. Preferred eating to moving.

GEMINI Butterfly. Brightly coloured and flappy.

CANCER Hen. Clucking over your chicks.

LEO Lion. Head of the pride.

VIRGO Bee. Industrious and task-focused.

PET HATES

LIBRA Golden retriever. Loyal and eager to please.

SCORPIO Wasp. Persistent and slightly scary.

SAGITTARIUS Wild horse. Untameable.

CAPRICORN Donkey. Hard-working and Eeyore-ish.

AQUARIUS Spider. Building the webs.

PISCES Seahorse. Gentle and strange.

PET HATES

What to avoid if you want to stay on their good side

ARIES Beating them at *anything*.

TAURUS Taking food off their plate.

GEMINI Withholding information.

CANCER Belittling their fears.

LEO Forgetting their name.

VIRGO Forcing them to do karaoke.

LIBRA Spilling red wine on their carpet.

SCORPIO Sleeping with their ex.

SAGITTARIUS Not inviting them to a party.

CAPRICORN Taking credit for their work.

AQUARIUS Beating them at Scrabble.

PISCES Criticising them for their vices.

GRUDGE MATCH

Will they hold it against you forever?

SCORPIO, TAURUS, CANCER

Yes. Until the end of time. If vengeance is not delivered, the grudge will be passed on to their children and grandchildren.

LEO, GEMINI, LIBRA

Yes, but not for long. A sincere apology should sort it out.

CAPRICORN, VIRGO

Not a grudge as such, but they are definitely keeping score. That black mark against you will come back and bite you in the ass one day.

ARIES, SAGITTARIUS, AQUARIUS, PISCES

No, it's not their style.

STRESS VS CHILL

Signs that need to relax

ARIES 'Fast' is your only speed.

GEMINI Streamline! One thing at a time…

VIRGO More delegate, less do.

SCORPIO Chill out and let a few things slide.

SAGITTARIUS Hold your horses! It's OK to stay in one place.

AQUARIUS Slow down and connect.

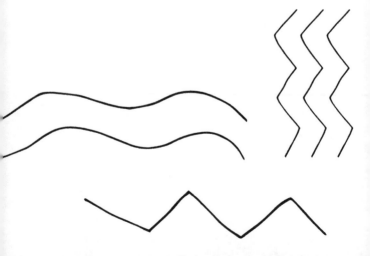

Signs that need to get out of the slow lane

TAURUS Less lounging, more action.

CANCER Stop worrying and get on with it.

LEO Less delegate, more do.

LIBRA Breaking a sweat occasionally won't kill you.

CAPRICORN Playing the long game doesn't have to mean moving slowly.

PISCES Getting out of bed would be a good start, Pisces . . .

MANAGE THE
MELTDOWN

And when it all feels too much, turn to the stars . . .

LEO, ARIES, SAGITTARIUS

Telling you to chill out would just light the blue touch paper.
Get out of the house, do some exercise. You'll be less furious
if you're exhausted.

TAURUS, VIRGO, CAPRICORN

Identify the problems, get organised, make a plan. And maybe
have a snack.

GEMINI, LIBRA, AQUARIUS

Talk to a friend, a colleague, or even the barista – you air signs need to talk it out. Get another perspective.

CANCER, SCORPIO, PISCES

Have a cry, find someone to hug, then ask yourself: is it really that bad?

PARTY TIME

What's your sign's perfect night out?

CANCER, VIRGO, SCORPIO

Getting the gang together. Catching up with old friends, preferably round someone's house.

TAURUS, CAPRICORN

Dinner out. A fun evening with a small group and some great food.

PISCES, LEO, LIBRA

House party! The more people the better. Must include dancing.

SAGITTARIUS, AQUARIUS, ARIES, GEMINI

An unpredictable adventure. Starts small but quickly grows to include random strangers, multiple cab rides, basement bars and waking up somewhere unexpected.

HOUSE PARTY
SURVIVAL GUIDE

How to have a night you can remember

ARIES Don't suggest a drinking game.

TAURUS Step away from the buffet.

GEMINI You don't have to talk to everyone in the room.

CANCER Co-ordinate with your crew and arrive together.

LEO Read your audience and know when to shut up!

VIRGO Try not to judge – even if it's not to your standards it might still be fun.

LIBRA Don't starve yourself just to preserve your lipstick.

SCORPIO Try a little mingling. No one's out to get you!

SAGITTARIUS No red wine in the living room, clumsy!

CAPRICORN Ditch the work, accept the invite and enjoy!

41

AQUARIUS Relax, you don't have to add these people to
your network.

PISCES Decide in advance how much to drink and stick to it.

10PM ON A NIGHT OUT WITH THE SIGNS

Where are they at?

ARIES Starting a fight.

TAURUS Next door at the kebab shop.

GEMINI Outside snogging someone.

CANCER Crying in the toilets.

LEO Still at home getting ready.

VIRGO Being put in a taxi home by their friends.

LIBRA Doing shots at the bar with randoms.

SCORPIO In the corner having a deep and meaningful.

SAGITTARIUS Looking for their lost coat and bag.

CAPRICORN Sitting at a table alone, judging people.

AQUARIUS Owning the dancefloor.

PISCES Smoking out the back.

TATTOOS

Who got inked?

ARIES Full sleeve.

TAURUS Something really tasteful, if at all.

GEMINI Something in Sanskrit you hope means what it's meant to.

CANCER Too afraid what your mum will say.

LEO Your own name.

VIRGO You say you want to, but secretly too scared of the pain.

LIBRA Stick to henna.

SCORPIO Your ex's name.

SAGITTARIUS A tiny bird on their ankle you got while travelling.

CAPRICORN No, not your style.

AQUARIUS Something cryptic you refuse to explain.

PISCES A line of poetry.

COSMIC HANGOVER CURES

What's in store and how to cope with it

	How you feel	What you need
ARIES	Is this a headache or is my head caving in?	Drink water and do some light exercise.
TAURUS	A bit dusty, but not too bad.	Have a massage, just to be sure.
GEMINI	Completely paranoid. Does everyone hate me?	Get out the house, find a yoga studio, calm down.
CANCER	Very, very emotional.	Watch *Titanic*.
LEO	Like thinking is much harder than usual.	Call a friend who will come and look after you.
VIRGO	Like there's a system malfunction.	Alphabetise your books.

	How you feel	What you need
LIBRA	Totally fine, honestly! Great!	Really, Libra? Start with a cup of tea.
SCORPIO	Existential. What is the point of it all?	Keep the curtains closed, watch *Friends*.
SAGITTARIUS	Confused. Where is my stuff? How did I get home?	Check for injuries. All good? Carry on.
CAPRICORN	A sense of impending doom.	Do some cathartic admin or build some shelves.
AQUARIUS	Annoyed by absolutely everything.	Go for a solo walk, avoid all Cancerians.
PISCES	Still drunk.	Stick to simple tasks. Resist the Bloody Mary.

DISNEY FILMS

Which classic speaks to your sign?

ARIES *Hercules.* Because the right workout saves the day.

TAURUS *The Jungle Book.* Baloo! Forget all those worries and strife!

GEMINI *Aladdin.* Geminis can't resist the fun and mercurial genie.

CANCER *The Little Mermaid.* Hidden depths and longing get Cancer every time. Plus, there's a crab in it.

LEO *The Lion King.* Natch! Simba must overcome adversity to get his power and everything he was born to be.

VIRGO *Cinderella.* Virgo wants to get the cleaning done AND go to the ball.

LIBRA *Beauty and the Beast.* Clever, kind girl cures angry, hairy guy and balance is restored.

SCORPIO *Frozen.* Because Scorpios sometimes feel like they live in an ice castle on their own.

SAGITTARIUS *Pocahontas.* Adventure! Discovery! Painting with the colours of the wind!

CAPRICORN *Snow White and the Seven Dwarfs.* The work ethic of those dwarfs really appeals.

AQUARIUS *Peter Pan.* All about the outsider maverick who doesn't want to grow up.

PISCES *Fantasia.* The only people who get this film are at least one of the following: art students/high/Pisces.

WHAT MAKES YOU CRY?

The thing your sign can't handle . . .

ARIES Losing.

TAURUS Sharing.

GEMINI Being confronted by someone equally smart.

CANCER Everything.

LEO Getting a huge zit.

VIRGO Lack of order.

48

LIBRA Injustice.

SCORPIO Losing control.

SAGITTARIUS Broken bones.

CAPRICORN Not getting the promotion.

AQUARIUS Nothing.

PISCES Cute animals; mean people.

AND WHAT WILL CHEER YOU UP?

Feel better.

ARIES Gunning for a new PB on your morning run.

TAURUS A trip to the big Waitrose.

GEMINI Writing a blog post.

CANCER Inviting your best friends round for homemade pizza.

LEO Getting your hair done.

VIRGO Reorganising your wardrobe.

LIBRA Planning some interior decorating.

SCORPIO Shopping for underwear.

SAGITTARIUS Buying some glossy travel magazines.

CAPRICORN Updating your impressive CV.

AQUARIUS Binge watching the latest cool documentary series.

PISCES Doing something kind for someone who's down.

NEW YEAR'S RESOLUTIONS

Be honest, what do you need to focus on this year?

ARIES Balancing your determination with respect for others.

TAURUS Being a little more flexible.

GEMINI Being honest about what you really want – with yourself and others.

CANCER Embracing the positive, letting the negative emotions go.

LEO Listening more to others.

VIRGO Believing in yourself – you CAN do this.

LIBRA Making decisions based on what YOU want (and standing by your choices).

SCORPIO Using your powers of intuition for personal transformation.

SAGITTARIUS Doing some career soul-searching – what do you really want from your job?

CAPRICORN Booking in some time off – and taking it!

AQUARIUS Making more time to connect and empathise with loved ones.

PISCES Deciding to do something and seeing it all the way through to the end.

NEW CHALLENGES

Try something different . . .

ARIES   Develop your side hustle.

TAURUS   Learn to play ukelele.

GEMINI   Write a book.

CANCER   Master cooking a new cuisine.

LEO   Get your paintbox out.

VIRGO   Go vegan.

LIBRA   Reinvent your wardrobe.

SCORPIO   Volunteer.

SAGITTARIUS   Pick something different to read.

CAPRICORN   Climb a mountain.

AQUARIUS   Join an improv group.

PISCES   Take a photo every day for a month.

ME TIME

How to take a break from everyone

ARIES Go for a run.

TAURUS Walk in the woods.

GEMINI Turn your phone off for 10 minutes.

CANCER Shut the kitchen door and bake a cake.

LEO Don your best pyjamas and watch a film.

VIRGO Meditate.

LIBRA Read a book.

SCORPIO Turn your phone off, stay at home.

SAGITTARIUS Go for a long drive.

CAPRICORN Spend some time with your online shares portfolio.

AQUARIUS Me time? Sounds boring.

PISCES Light a candle and look at some crystals.

COSMIC COMFORT FOOD

Treats for all!

ARIES Nachos, extra chilli.

TAURUS A big plate of pasta, just the way you like it.

GEMINI Haribo.

CANCER Ice cream.

LEO An exotic cocktail, beautifully served.

VIRGO Home-made soup.

LIBRA Sharing platter.

SCORPIO Steak and chips, rare.

SAGITTARIUS All-you-can-eat buffet.

CAPRICORN Bone broth.

AQUARIUS Ice-cream-filled doughnut.

PISCES Vodka, gin, wine ...

PERFECT HOLIDAY

Your dream getaway

ARIES   Fitness bootcamp by the Med or skiing in the Alps.

TAURUS   Camping somewhere wild – New Zealand or Montana.

GEMINI   A city close to the beach. Variety! Barcelona or LA.

CANCER   Holiday camp with the fam, South of France.

LEO   A 7* hotel in Positano so you can strut your stuff.

VIRGO   Staycation.

LIBRA   Boutique bouji hotel in Dubrovnik or Stockholm.

SCORPIO   Mexico City for the Day of the Dead festival.

SAGITTARIUS   Somewhere far away, exotic and adventurous – Himalayas or Polynesian islands.

CAPRICORN   Everest base camp.

AQUARIUS   Somewhere you can be useful – help build an eco school.

PISCES   All-inclusive hotel in Marrakesh or Thailand.

FESTIVAL VIBES

Where will you be this summer?

PISCES, TAURUS, CANCER

Glastonbury. Dancing in the mud in day-glo body paint and fairy wings.

LEO, SAGITTARIUS, ARIES

Coachella. You've been planning your outfits since last year.

GEMINI, AQUARIUS, CAPRICORN

The Edinburgh Fringe Festival. Or Hay-on-Wye. Anywhere you can binge on culture and feel clever.

VIRGO, SCORPIO, LIBRA

Cannes Film Festival. Celebrities and free canapés are a requirement.

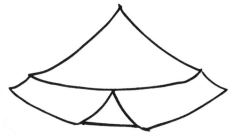

<u>HALLOWEEN</u>

What's your sign's dressing-up style?

SCORPIO, LEO, CAPRICORN

Sexy witch, sexy zombie nurse, sexy superhero, sexy cat ...

CANCER, VIRGO, LIBRA

No effort bedsheet ghost, toilet-paper mummy, badly drawn skeleton.

ARIES, GEMINI, SAGITTARIUS

All about the LOLs as a retro children's TV character or giant vegetable.

PISCES, TAURUS, AQUARIUS

Detailed and realistic Amy Winehouse, Vegas Elvis, Elizabeth I, the TARDIS

BIRTHDAY TREATS

What to give them . . .

ARIES A trip to Laser Quest.

TAURUS Something small but luxurious.

GEMINI A massive bag of pick 'n' mix.

CANCER A cheesemaking workshop.

LEO A huge party.

VIRGO Complete control over the whole day.

LIBRA Designer accessories – a scarf or sunglasses.

SCORPIO A black leather bag (with lots of compartments).

SAGITTARIUS Tickets to a gig.

CAPRICORN A watch.

AQUARIUS A donation to their favourite charity.

PISCES A gong bath.

SNACKS

How to resist those bad habits

	What you want	Try
ARIES	Too busy to snack!	A muesli bar – easy to eat on the go.
TAURUS	Some of everything please.	Portion control.
GEMINI	All snacks, no meals.	Having set mealtimes.
CANCER	Cream cakes.	Sorbet – still feels like a treat.
LEO	Expensive treats.	Picking one thing and having a little bit of it every day.

	What you want	Try
VIRGO	To give up carbs.	A little of what you want.
LIBRA	What everyone else has.	A beautiful fruit platter.
SCORPIO	Something spicy or unusual.	Wasabi peas, jalapeño cheese.
SAGITTARIUS	Pina colada on a tropical beach.	Coconut chips.
CAPRICORN	To wait until dinnertime.	Some trail mix to keep your energy up.
AQUARIUS	Something different.	Carob chocolate, beef jerky.
PISCES	Some peanuts with your wine.	How about just the peanuts?

WHICH HARRY POTTER CHARACTER ARE YOU?

ARIES Fred and George Weasley; entrepreneurial and self-determining.

TAURUS Pomona Sprout; as Professor of Herbology, she knows her plants.

GEMINI Nymphadora Tonks; mercurial and changes appearance in the blink of an eye.

CANCER Dobby the House Elf; caring and loyal, but emotional and unpredictable.

LEO Harry Potter; always the star of the show!

VIRGO Hermione Granger; her time turner means she can cram more hours into the day.

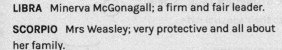

LIBRA Minerva McGonagall; a firm and fair leader.

SCORPIO Mrs Weasley; very protective and all about her family.

SAGITTARIUS Hagrid; a half giant who's always putting his foot in it.

CAPRICORN Snape; depressive tendencies and duty bound till the end.

AQUARIUS Arthur Weasley; obsessed with Muggle 'tech' such as plugs.

PISCES Ron Weasley; sensitive and emotionally volatile.

HOROSCOPE HACKS

How to . . .

DEAL WITH ARIES' TEMPER TANTRUM:
Sit it out, they'll get over it eventually.

CHANGE STUBBORN TAURUS' MIND:
Appeal to their sensual side.

SLOW DOWN GEMINI:
Dangle a carrot that makes them focus.

CRITICISE CANCER:
Very, very gently. Or just don't.

MAKE LEO PULL THEIR WEIGHT:
Reassure them they are brilliant and talented at the task in hand.

CONVINCE VIRGO TO LET THINGS GO:
Distract them by asking for advice on another problem.

STOP LIBRA SPENDING MONEY:

Convince them that budgeting now means more luxury treats in the future.

ENCOURAGE SCORPIO TO OPEN UP:

They will have to really trust you (or be planning to kill you after).

GET SAGITTARIUS TO FACE FACTS:

Get them somewhere with no distractions – and keep it positive.

STOP CAPRICORN WORKING SO HARD:

'You know, even Mark Zuckerberg takes holidays . . .'

MAKE AQUARIUS PLAN:

Use logic to explain why boundaries can actually create more freedom.

BRING PISCES BACK DOWN TO EARTH:

Appeal to their wise side or tell them you need their help.

SKILL SWAP

Which star sign could you learn from?

ARIES BE MORE TAURUS

A bit of patience never hurt anyone – get in line!

TAURUS BE MORE GEMINI

Conversation is key.

GEMINI BE MORE CANCER

Make more time for those you love.

CANCER BE MORE LEO

Show off what you're great at.

LEO BE MORE VIRGO

Let someone else have the limelight for a change.

VIRGO BE MORE LIBRA

Aim for balance – you need to relax sometimes.

LIBRA BE MORE ARIES

It's important to put yourself first.

SCORPIO BE MORE SAGITTARIUS

Holding a grudge is tiring – let it go.

SAGITTARIUS BE MORE CAPRICORN

Develop your work ethic, even if it seems boring.

CAPRICORN BE MORE AQUARIUS

Co-operate – working together makes us stronger.

AQUARIUS BE MORE PISCES

Listen to your instincts and follow your gut.

PISCES BE MORE SCORPIO

Committing to something can feel magical too.

WHAT'S YOUR SUPERPOWER?

And are you using it to its full potential?

ARIES Leader. The other signs will follow wherever you take them.

TAURUS Connoisseur. You have the recommendations.

GEMINI Connector. You always know just the right person to ask ...

CANCER Nurturer. You make people feel understood.

LEO Social glue. You bring people together – and throw legendary parties!

VIRGO Organiser. You make sure everything is done right.

LIBRA Charmer. You turn on your sunny smile and get what you want.

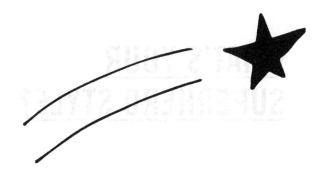

SCORPIO Detective. You can get to the bottom of a situation and sort it.

SAGITTARIUS Adventurer. Any trip with you can turn into an amazing journey.

CAPRICORN Survivor. Everyone wants you on their team in the tough times.

AQUARIUS Innovator. You're always ahead of the curve.

PISCES Healer. Calm, wise and kind, you make sad people feel better.

WHAT'S YOUR
SUPERHERO STYLE?

GEMINI, SCORPIO, CAPRICORN

Batman. You do good deeds, but only by night and in disguise.
Otherwise it would totally ruin your image.

SAGITTARIUS, ARIES, AQUARIUS

Catwoman. Sure, you'll swoop in and defeat the bad guys.
But really it's just a great excuse to wear a cool outfit.

TAURUS, LEO, LIBRA

Superman. You love wearing a cape, the bigger and
swishier the better. You are brave, heroic and you'd like
a big round of applause please.

CANCER, VIRGO, PISCES

Wonder Woman. You definitely want to end all war, and you
can talk to animals (at least, you're sure you know what your
cat is thinking).

STAR STYLE

What should you wear today?

ARIES Your sign is associated with fiery red, though you see things in black and white. Monochrome is a strong look for you.

TAURUS You're all about beauty and comfort, and textures are very important. Go for earthy colours and natural fibres.

GEMINI Don't be afraid to try out new things. You can wear almost anything and you're the master at changing it up.

CANCER Seek out soft and comfortable fabrics, and rummage for vintage treasure – you like things with a history.

LEO You always know how to get noticed! Even without the bright colours and directional outfits you usually go for.

VIRGO Go for minimal, clean lines and crisp colours. You have a real eye for quality brands.

LIBRA All about harmony! You trust your own sense of style and don't care about the latest trends.

SCORPIO Go back to black. Whether it's a swipe of eyeliner, a biker boot or a smart tuxedo jacket, you're happiest when you feel powerful and sexy.

SAGITTARIUS No one ever accuses you of being a wallflower! Embrace your love of bright colours, pattern and anything exotic.

CAPRICORN You're most comfortable when there's a dress code, and always smartly turned out. Go for great tailoring that never goes out of style.

AQUARIUS Naturally unconventional and rebellious in your style, avoid anything fussy or flouncy – it'll just annoy you.

PISCES Your creativity often means you have your own unique sense of style – so embrace it and wear what makes you feel good.

<u>ACCESSORISE</u>

What completes your perfect outfit?

ARIES Rules the head, you can really rock a hat.

TAURUS All about the neck and shoulders, reach for a statement necklace or collar.

GEMINI Rules the hands, grab a glittering cocktail ring.

CANCER Think moon-like tones of white, pearl and silver.

LEO Ruled by the sun, buy some golden bling and shine!

VIRGO Your sign is all about legs. Show yours off in a mini skirt or perfectly cut trousers.

LIBRA Ruled by Venus, and all about balance. Go for subtle accents, not statement pieces.

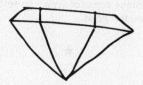

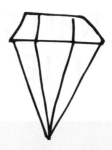

SCORPIO Your sign is all about keeping it incognito. Work your trademark black shades.

SAGITTARIUS Your sign's sexiness comes from the hips and ass. Grab a cool belt to accentuate your assets!

CAPRICORN Your sign is associated with great teeth or bone structure. Keep accessories classic and let your natural gifts shine!

AQUARIUS Ruled by Saturn and Uranus, your sign is ahead of its time, so go for unusual, unconventional pieces.

PISCES Rules the feet, you need a great pair of shoes.

WHAT'S YOUR HOME STYLE?

ARIES Black and white, functional and practical.

TAURUS Raw oak table, greens and neutral tones, super comfy sofa.

GEMINI Always moving things around and redecorating, very up-to-date.

CANCER Full of photos of the people you love; the big kitchen has a huge table and well-stocked fridge.

LEO GLAM! Gilded picture frames and a bright, bold living room.

VIRGO Minimal, and always spotless. Storage solutions that would impress NASA.

LIBRA The interior designer of the zodiac, everything is in harmony and balance with a neatness and style.

SCORPIO Essentially functional but crammed with books and magazines.

SAGITTARIUS Full of colour and magical items you've collected on your travels.

CAPRICORN Classic and traditional, with a study. The lounge is smarter than it is comfortable.

AQUARIUS Lighting, heat and music is controlled from an iPad. Painted in light blue hues; the kitchen has never been used.

PISCES Great sound system. Cool Polaroid snaps stuck up on the walls.

WHO'S YOUR CELEBRITY TWIN?

ARIES Motivated and determined: Robert Downey Jr., Keira Knightley.

TAURUS Stunning and reliable: George Clooney, Penélope Cruz.

GEMINI Unpredictable and witty: Russell Brand, Helena Bonham Carter.

CANCER The boy/girl next door: Tom Hanks, Margot Robbie.

LEO Cool and stylish: Shawn Mendes, Jennifer Lopez.

VIRGO Cute and nerdy: Amy Poehler, Liam Payne.

LIBRA Famous for being in power couples: John Lennon, Catherine Zeta-Jones.

SCORPIO Sexy AF: Ryan Gosling, Kendall Jenner.

SAGITTARIUS High octane: Jay Z, Nicki Minaj.

CAPRICORN Classic beauties: Brad Pitt, Kate Middleton.

AQUARIUS Down-to-earth and humanitarian: Ed Sheeran, Amal Clooney.

PISCES Artistic and emotional: Chris Martin, Rihanna.

LOVE LOVE LOVE

LOVE

LOVE

LOVE

L

LOV

LOVE

LOVE

LOVE

LOVED UP

LOVE LOVE LOVE LOVE LOVE LOVE LOVE

SNOG, MARRY, AVOID

snog

Perfect for no-strings fun

Aries + Leo = 😗

Taurus + Sagittarius = 😗

Gemini + Aquarius = 😗

Cancer + Capricorn = 😗

Virgo + Pisces = 😗

Libra + Scorpio = 😗

m a r r y

Dream teams 4-ever!

Aries + Libra = ♡

Sagittarius + Leo = ♡

Gemini + Aquarius = ♡

Cancer + Capricorn = ♡

Taurus + Scorpio = ♡

Virgo + Pisces = ♡

a v o i d

Never say never, but these
do not work on paper . . .

Aries + Virgo = ⊘

Taurus + Libra = ⊘

Gemini + Pisces = ⊘

Cancer + Leo = ⊘

Aquarius + Capricorn = ⊘

Sagittarius + Scorpio = ⊘

SIGNS TO SWIPE RIGHT

ARIES–LIBRA:

A dynamic duo who like to put the world to rights.
Chilled-out Libra will let Aries win, while Aries will bring the
decisiveness that Libra lacks.

TAURUS–SCORPIO:

These signs provide the genuine loyalty that they both crave.
Plus, sensual Taurus will enjoy wordless passion with intense
Scorpio.

GEMINI–SAGITTARIUS:

An endlessly curious and sociable couple.
Both these signs value freedom and real friendship.
They know how to communicate and when to give each
other space.

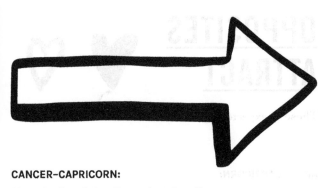

CANCER–CAPRICORN:

Shared values bring these signs together.
They know what's important to them and work hard to build
a successful home and business.

LEO–AQUARIUS:

This sociable pair love to work the room.
These signs know how to enjoy themselves. They both love
getting attention, but aren't usually jealous.

VIRGO–PISCES:

A kind and caring pair who look after each other.
Responsible Virgo will watch out for dreamy Pisces, who
brings the wisdom and intuition that Virgo can lack.

OPPOSITES ATTRACT

These unexpected celestial matches can really work

ARIES–CAPRICORN:

Though Capricorn lacks Aries' fiery optimism, they share Aries' ambition. This pair can really spur each other on.

TAURUS–SAGITTARIUS:

Sagittarius' passion for travel and adventure can freak out home-loving Taurus. However, they both love the great outdoors and their different perspectives can be mutually supportive.

GEMINI–VIRGO:

These two signs are ruled by the planet Mercury. Their need to communicate means they will WhatsApp each other day and night. Practical Virgo can help Gemini focus their brilliant mind.

THE BEST AND WORST
SITS OF DATING YE

CANCER–AQUARIUS:

Curious Aquarius is fascinated by Cancer's depth of emotion.
Cancer's natural talent to nurture can make these different
signs oddly compatible.

LEO–SCORPIO:

Scorpio's sex appeal draws the attention of glamour-
loving Leo. These signs are prone to jealousy and
possessiveness, so trust is key. Not always an easy
match, but a truly passionate pairing.

LIBRA–PISCES:

Ever-accommodating Libra and dream-weaving Pisces like
things idealistically beautiful, with Libra enjoying the artistic,
mystical nature of their Pisces pals.

THE BEST AND WORST BITS OF DATING THE SIGNS

ARIES Very fun, BUT prone to losing their temper.

TAURUS Patient, BUT mind-bogglingly stubborn.

GEMINI Very witty, BUT too chatty first thing in the morning.

CANCER Sweet and considerate, BUT capable of sulking for days.

LEO Generous, BUT has a GIANT ego.

VIRGO Prepared to do anything for you, BUT sometimes fussy and critical.

LIBRA   The social glue, BUT a terrible devil's advocate.

SCORPIO   Passionate, BUT prone to playing mind games.

SAGITTARIUS   Always open to new experiences, BUT a
complete know-it-all.

CAPRICORN   Reliable and trustworthy, BUT often pessimistic.

AQUARIUS   Ingenious, BUT unlikely to change their point of
view for anyone.

PISCES   Enchanting, BUT prone to flights of fantasy.

HOW TO GET YOUR CRUSH'S ATTENTION

ARIES Show off at sport.

TAURUS Send them flowers.

GEMINI Name drop.

CANCER Show them you love children.

LEO Look amazing.

VIRGO Open up about a problem and let them help you.

LIBRA Feed them some fun and flirtatious chat-up lines.

SCORPIO Make eye contact but say nothing.

SAGITTARIUS Make them laugh.

CAPRICORN Ask them about their job.

AQUARIUS Make friends with their friends.

PISCES Talk to them about the meaning of life.

LOVED UP

How to be in a relationship with the signs

ARIES Keep the adventure alive and the fire going.

TAURUS Spoil them so they know they are special.

GEMINI Communicate! In all ways – and not just when you want them to buy milk.

CANCER Eat together to stay together. And Cancers need lots of hugs.

LEO Date night is mandatory! And dress up – even if you stay in.

VIRGO Love a comfortable routine. Always let them know if you're going to be late.

LIBRA It's all about the partnership. Don't shut them out.

SCORPIO Show them you are committed. Scorpios want to know how you feel.

SAGITTARIUS Want to be loved, but also value their independence. Don't clip their wings.

CAPRICORN It's all about mutual admiration and respect in this partnership.

AQUARIUS Be their best friend as well as their SO.

PISCES Don't let life admin take over – romance is key for dreamy Pisces.

WHAT'S YOUR SIGN'S DATING STYLE?

TAURUS, CAPRICORN, LIBRA

Would send a first message that just says 'Hey!'

ARIES, LEO, SAGITTARIUS, SCORPIO, GEMINI

Has an active profile on most dating apps.

GEMINI, SCORPIO, VIRGO

Internet stalks – sorry, 'researches' – anyone they fancy even a bit.

PISCES, CANCER, SAGITTARIUS

Imagines a whole future together before even going on a date.

HEY!

GEMINI, AQUARIUS, PISCES

Sends loads of flirty messages but hardly ever follows
through with a date.

SCORPIO, LIBRA

Uses a fake name online; lies about their age.

LEO, GEMINI, SAGITTARIUS

Swipes right on almost everyone to get the maximum
attention.

GEMINI, AQUARIUS, PISCES

Will ghost you without warning.

THEIR MESSAGING STYLE

When will they reply?

ARIES, GEMINI, SAGITTARIUS

Straight away – even if awaiting major surgery, at a funeral, or on a date with someone else.

VIRGO, TAURUS, AQUARIUS

Whenever they happen to see the message and have time – it wouldn't occur to them to play games.

LEO, SCORPIO, CANCER

Waits exactly the same amount of time that elapsed between their last message and your reply, plus one hour.

LIBRA, CAPRICORN

As long as it takes to compose the wittiest, most impressive response.

PISCES

Never.

THE PERFECT DATE

TAURUS–VIRGO, SAGITTARIUS–LIBRA
Picnic in the park.

ARIES–LEO, SCORPIO–AQUARIUS
Zip-lining.

CANCER–PISCES, LEO–LIBRA
Pizza-making class.

AQUARIUS–GEMINI, SAGITTARIUS–ARIES

Escape room.

LIBRA–CAPRICORN, PISCES–CANCER

Art gallery.

PISCES–SAGITTARIUS, GEMINI–LEO

Karaoke.

BLIND DATE

UNDERLINE

Should you let your friends set you up?

GEMINI, SAGITTARIUS, ARIES, LIBRA

Yes! You love meeting new people and your friends will pick someone great.

VIRGO, AQUARIUS, LEO, PISCES

Maybe. Is this a friend you trust? Choose a venue where you feel comfortable (don't drink too much!) and you'll probably have fun.

TAURUS, CAPRICORN, CANCER, SCORPIO

No. Could you meet them at a gig, as part of a group, or maybe your friends could introduce you at a party? Somewhere where there's less pressure.

DATING DEAL-BREAKERS

What will make the signs call the whole thing off?

ARIES Turning up late.

TAURUS Changing plans at the last minute.

GEMINI No sense of humour.

CANCER Being criticised.

LEO Scruffy or bad dresser.

VIRGO Bad breath.

LIBRA Rudeness.

SCORPIO Any indication of being hung up on an ex.

SAGITTARIUS Not owning a passport.

CAPRICORN Laziness.

AQUARIUS Being conventional.

PISCES Animal cruelty.

HOW TO CALM THOSE FIRST DATE NERVES

Even when it's awks

ARIES Resist the urge to dominate the situation because you're desperate to make a good first impression.

TAURUS If there's any sign that can handle a silence without it being awkward, it's you! Put your date to the test.

GEMINI Even if it's not the perfect date, you always relish the chance to meet someone new.

CANCER Pick somewhere with great food. Then you won't care so much if the date is bad.

LEO You live to tell your life story, but be sure to ask a few questions!

VIRGO You'll feel much calmer if you pick somewhere you've been before, so at least the venue is familiar.

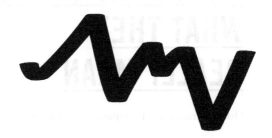

LIBRA Resist going into a full-on charm offensive – you don't have to make them fall in love with you straight away.

SCORPIO Take time to get to know them before you make up your mind. Immediate seduction is not essential.

SAGITTARIUS Try to keep some cards close to your chest. Your honesty is admirable, but you don't have to share everything!

CAPRICORN Go with the right attitude, don't decide it's a disaster before you even get there!

AQUARIUS Take it slowly and be alert to non-visual clues. Try not to mix up friendship and attraction.

PISCES Don't drink too much and don't take an off-the-cuff comment to heart – remember they might be nervous, too.

WHAT THEY SAY VS WHAT THEY REALLY MEAN

How to translate the signs in a relationship

	They say	They mean
ARIES	I can't wait to spend the rest of my life with you.	I want us to be the best couple ever.
TAURUS	I love you so much.	You're mine and I'm not sharing.
GEMINI	I'm not looking for anything serious, I enjoy dating.	I'm deeply insecure and hedging my bets.
CANCER	It's fine, don't worry about me.	I will never ever forgive you for this.
LEO	You're so gorge, I'm so proud of you.	You're almost as great as me!

	They say	They mean
VIRGO	Shall I help you with that?	You're definitely going to balls this up.
LIBRA	I don't mind, you decide.	You make a suggestion and I'll offer an alternative that will be our final choice.
SCORPIO	I love you.	Don't. Ever. Leave. Me.
SAGITTARIUS	You don't mind if I pop out for a drink with the gang?	Never come between me and my friends.
CAPRICORN	I'm just not that romantic.	I'm dying to love you but don't know how to tell you.
AQUARIUS	Thanks for being such a brilliant friend.	I'm in love with you but I haven't figured it out yet.
PISCES	I've never felt this way before.	It might change tomorrow, but I really mean it today.

VALENTINE'S DAY

Which signs are on board with the day of love?

SCORPIO, AQUARIUS

Hates it – Thinks it's a crass commercialisation of love.

CAPRICORN, CANCER, VIRGO

Pretends to hate it – Because they think no one will get
them anything.

TAURUS, GEMINI

Indifferent – Will stretch to a takeaway and a bottle of wine.

LIBRA, PISCES, SAGITTARIUS, ARIES, LEO

LOVES it – Will do chocolates, restaurants, flowers ...
the works.

HOW TO CHARM THEM

What every sign most wants to hear

ARIES You're the best.

TAURUS Let's go for a walk.

GEMINI That's my favourite book, too!

CANCER I'd love to meet your family one day.

LEO You look amazing.

VIRGO Will you come to Wholefoods with me?

LIBRA How can you possibly be single?

SCORPIO *Hold eye contact to let them know they're the most important person in the room*

SAGITTARIUS You really inspire me!

CAPRICORN I can see you're really going places.

AQUARIUS Is that the latest iPhone?

PISCES I feel like we've met in a former life.

MINI BREAK

Whisk them away on the perfect romantic weekend

ARIES A whistle-stop trip to Dubai.

TAURUS A treehouse eco hotel.

GEMINI The latest hot city destination where all the cool cats are hanging.

CANCER Venice, connected and watery.

LEO A luxury spa in the Cotswolds.

VIRGO A foodie trip to Copenhagen.

LIBRA Somewhere beachy and sophisticated.

SCORPIO Somewhere old and mysterious, like Budapest or Prague.

SAGITTARIUS Iceland, to see the Northern Lights.

CAPRICORN Skiing in Switzerland.

AQUARIUS Clubbing in Berlin.

PISCES Somewhere quaint by the sea, Cornwall or Brittany.

MEET THE PARENTS

When will they introduce you?

CANCER, VIRGO

Immediately. There probably won't even be a second date unless Mum or Dad approves.

TAURUS, ARIES, LEO, PISCES

Pretty soon. They're close to at least some of their family, and don't think it's a big deal to invite you to a get-together.

CAPRICORN, LIBRA

A formal meeting will be called after no fewer than eight months. It may feel like some kind of summit or ambassador's reception. Expect to be told what to wear.

SCORPIO, AQUARIUS, SAGITTARIUS, GEMINI

Maybe never. Either they are hiding something, or they think their parents are boring and will undermine their roguish air of mystery.

PUT A RING ON IT

How will the signs pop the question?

ARIES On the big screen at a sporting event.

TAURUS On a picnic.

GEMINI With a very clever and elaborate surprise proposal.

CANCER At home with rose petals everywhere.

LEO With a brass band flash mob.

VIRGO After thinking about it for months, and only when sure of the answer.

LIBRA In Paris, at sunset.

SCORPIO Declaring their eternal love with candles and dramatic music.

SAGITTARIUS With an extravagant display of affection.

CAPRICORN A traditional proposal, down on one knee with their grandmother's ring.

AQUARIUS Only if they believe death to be imminent.

PISCES By reading you a poem they wrote (while crying).

WEDDING ETIQUETTE

Will they behave on your big day?

ARIES Makes an impromptu speech.

TAURUS Completely focused on the canapés.

GEMINI Talks to everyone.

CANCER Drunk and tearful by 4pm.

LEO Buys the perfect gift.

VIRGO Buys the cheapest gift.

LIBRA Flirts with your dad.

SCORPIO Snogs the best man/bridesmaid.

SAGITTARIUS Owns the dance floor.

CAPRICORN Makes sure everyone gets their taxi at the end.

AQUARIUS Does shots at the bar with your weird uncle.

PISCES Falls asleep during the speeches.

EVER BEEN TEMPTED TO CHEAT?

ARIES You love the chase but you don't have to catch 'em all!

TAURUS Your loyalty is the best thing about you.

GEMINI It crosses your mind all the time, but you know you don't have to act on it.

CANCER Only when you feel threatened. Looking elsewhere isn't going to help.

LEO If pride is the issue, remember how much you love your pack.

VIRGO You sometimes think about it, but it feels too scary a leap.

LIBRA You're naturally flirtatious, but try to rein it in.

SCORPIO Is it really a deep karmic connection you're feeling, or do you just want to get into their pants?

SAGITTARIUS You're a natural thrill-seeker, but resist taking every opportunity for a new adventure.

CAPRICORN Absolutely not.

AQUARIUS No, you are freedom-loving but always loyal.

PISCES Not for shallow reasons, but Pisceans are capable of being in love with more than person . . .

FLIRTING OR FRIEND ZONE?

How to tell if they are crushing on you

ARIES They'll tell you!

TAURUS They've made a big effort to look great.

GEMINI Asks you 5,327 questions.

CANCER Offers to cook for you.

LEO Makes you the centre of their attention.

VIRGO Tries to look after you.

LIBRA Will stay in your orbit, subtly trying to attract your attention.

SCORPIO You feel them looking at you a *lot.*

SAGITTARIUS They laugh at everything you say.

CAPRICORN They completely ignore you.

AQUARIUS They try to make friends with you.

PISCES They tell you stories.

HOW THEY END IT

What's their break-up style?

ARIES Crystal-clear ending.

TAURUS Cries and hates every second of it.

GEMINI Cheats so they get dumped.

CANCER Sits them down and tells them it's over.

LEO Takes them to dinner.

VIRGO Gives a well-planned speech.

LIBRA 'It's not you, it's me.'

SCORPIO Becomes cold and distant.

SAGITTARIUS Is a little too honest.

CAPRICORN Writes a heartfelt letter.

AQUARIUS 'I think we'd be better as friends.'

PISCES Ghosts them.

HOW TO SURVIVE A BREAK-UP

	What you do	Try
ARIES	Get angry and swear lots.	Prioritising exercise, looking hot, going out.
TAURUS	Refuse to move on and wait for them to return.	Broadening your horizons and seeing how many amazing people are out there.
GEMINI	Try to stay friends (and friends with their friends).	Meeting some new pals.
CANCER	Stay at home, cry, look at photos.	Chucking out their stuff and seeing the people you love.
LEO	Feel like you've lost your spark.	Spending time with people who appreciate your sense of fun.
VIRGO	Feel anxious and stressed.	Practising some yoga and eating properly.

	What you do	Try
LIBRA	Immediately start dating again.	Spending some time alone, getting to know what you like, seeing your friends.
SCORPIO	Burn all their stuff, vow to never love again.	Keeping your heart open (you thrive during difficult times).
SAGITTARIUS	Decide to up sticks and leave.	Going on holiday first before selling the house.
CAPRICORN	Descend into a period of depression.	Focusing on keeping your spirits high, but appreciate the wisdom you are gaining, even if it's crippling.
AQUARIUS	Pretend it's not happening.	Talking it over with friends to process what happened.
PISCES	Dwell on the past and cry.	Throwing a pity party, then channelling your pain into your art.

HOW TO BE SINGLE

Embrace your freedom

ARIES Be brave! Try going out alone and see who you run into...

TAURUS Take some time out. Live in your PJs, eat cake and relax.

GEMINI Meet as many new people as possible. Get out there and join some clubs (or just go clubbing).

CANCER Spend more time with besties and the family.

LEO Buy a new outfit. Enjoy ALL THE ATTENTION. Indulge in guilt-free flirting!

VIRGO Relish the chance to set up weekly routines without having to consider someone else's plans.

LIBRA Ask your mates to set you up or go online; aim for one date a week!

SCORPIO This is a good time to get to know your most intimate self. Perhaps explore therapy or a mindfulness course?

SAGITTARIUS V O Y A G E. Go somewhere new every day, even if it's just a street you've never walked down before.

CAPRICORN Focus on the next career move – let your ambition become your main priority for a while.

AQUARIUS Take stock of your values – does your lifestyle mirror what you love? If not, change it up.

PISCES Have fun, but don't go OTT on drinking and partying. It might also be time to meditate and reconnect with your creative self.

WORK

WORK

WORK

WORK

WORK

WORK

WORK

WORK

WORK

WORK

BOSSING IT

WORK

WORK

WORK

WORK

WORK STYLE

Can you adapt your work to suit your sign?

VIRGO, TAURUS, LEO

Nine-to-Five – The Monday-to-Friday vibe works just fine for you. You like structure and routine, and having the weekend off to recharge.

GEMINI, LIBRA, PISCES

Flexi – You generally like being in the office, but you want to be able to duck out early when you fancy it.

CAPRICORN, CANCER, SAGITTARIUS

Remote Working – You are more productive if you can be left alone to do your own thing, though you still like being able to dial into calls and bounce ideas off your colleagues.

AQUARIUS, SCORPIO, ARIES

Freelance – Freedom, being your own boss, sticking it to The Man – this is the way to go for you.

YOUR COLLEAGUES
LOVE YOU FOR ...

ARIES Getting things off the ground.

TAURUS Being utterly reliable.

GEMINI Blitzing out an article in 30 minutes.

CANCER Being a listening ear.

LEO Your super-sharp presentation skills.

VIRGO Being on top of everything, hitting deadlines.

LIBRA Charming everyone and closing the sale.

SCORPIO Pulling an all-nighter to get the project finished.

SAGITTARIUS Lightening the mood and envisioning new goals.

CAPRICORN Keeping a clear head under pressure.

AQUARIUS Facilitating a team effort.

PISCES Your amazing design and presentation skills.

WHAT INSPIRES YOU AT WORK

GEMINI, SAGITTARIUS

Solving a problem.

ARIES, SCORPIO, LEO

Beating the competition.

CAPRICORN, LEO, TAURUS, CANCER

A hefty bonus.

VIRGO, CANCER, PISCES

Helping people.

SCORPIO, PISCES

Achieving perfection.

AQUARIUS, ARIES, GEMINI

Making something brand new.

LIBRA, TAURUS, LEO

Making something beautiful.

MONEY . . .

ARIES Is the prize.

TAURUS Makes me feel great.

GEMINI Slips through my fingers.

CANCER Makes me feel secure.

LEO Pays for fun.

VIRGO Is for saving.

LIBRA Buys beautiful things.

SCORPIO Is all I think about.

SAGITTARIUS Brings freedom.

CAPRICORN Denotes success.

AQUARIUS Is the capitalist yoke.

PISCES Beer tokens.

TURN MONDAYS ⇒ MON-YAYS

Strategies for getting through the worst day of the week.

ARIES Start on Sunday to get ahead.

TAURUS Bring lots of lovely snacks. Go slowly.

GEMINI Plan drinks for Thursday. Tackle one task at a time.

CANCER Devise a plan, avoid communication.

LEO Tell everyone about your weekend. Oh look, it's lunch-time already!

VIRGO You're the most organised sign so Monday = no problem. Learn to say no, avoid doing everyone else's work today.

LIBRA Wear a great outfit. Make calls and build your network.

SCORPIO Enjoy all the gossip from the weekend.

SAGITTARIUS Book a holiday. Identify a project that involves a secondment to Barbados.

CAPRICORN LOVE Mondays!

AQUARIUS Ignore everyone. Escape outside at lunch.

PISCES Arrive late. Bring crystals.

THE COSMIC COMMUTE

Make the most of your journey to work

ARIES Run or cycle to work and arrive buzzing.

TAURUS Apply aromatherapy oils and give yourself time to meditate and relax.

GEMINI Books and podcasts will improve your morning.

CANCER Caffè latte and a pastry en route will ease you into the day.

LEO Choose a gym close to work where you can shower and preen, so you rock up looking fresh.

VIRGO Avoid the temptation to start working en route and practise mindfulness.

LIBRA Use the time to plan your day ahead.

SCORPIO Get up very early to avoid the rush hour and having to share your personal space.

SAGITTARIUS Read the paper and get a global perspective.

125

CAPRICORN You've already got the most efficient route down, and the journey timed to the second.

AQUARIUS Look around and get your kicks people-watching.

PISCES Listen to music, this is your time.

WORST-CASE WORK SCENARIOS

What brings your sign out in hives?

AQUARIUS, CAPRICORN, ARIES, SCORPIO

Compulsory organised fun.

TAURUS, VIRGO

Role play.

PISCES, SCORPIO, LIBRA

Performance reviews.

VIRGO, CANCER

Presenting in a meeting.

AQUARIUS, PISCES, LEO

People who use terms like 'onboarding' and 'circle back'.

SAGITTARIUS, TAURUS, CANCER

Excel spreadsheets.

LEO, SAGITTARIUS, LIBRA, CAPRICORN, ARIES

Being micro-managed.

YOUR COSMIC CAREER COACH

Love what you do, do what you love

ARIES You make things happen! Start your own business. *Role model: Victoria Beckham.*

TAURUS You make practical things beautiful. Become an architect, chef, designer. *Role model: Donatella Versace.*

GEMINI You connect people and ideas. You're a natural journalist, vlogger, talent scout. *Role model: Kanye West.*

CANCER You love to help things grow – nurture future minds as a school teacher or make money as a hedge fund manager. *Role model: Arianna Huffington.*

LEO You speak and everyone listens. You're a great team leader, actor, teacher. *Role model: Barack Obama.*

VIRGO You're super organised and the backbone of any office, organisation or, er, dictatorship. *Role model: Sheryl Sandberg.*

LIBRA You're a natural negotiator. How about politics, sales, front of house? *Role model: Cardi B.*

SCORPIO You're so full of energy and drive that you excel at anything you want badly enough. *Role model: Emma Stone.*

SAGITTARIUS You love feeling free and using your creative skills. Think about jobs where you can freelance, travel or live overseas. *Role model: Taylor Swift.*

CAPRICORN You're an ambitious high-flyer. Work for large organisations where you can climb the ladder. *Role model: Jeff Bezos.*

AQUARIUS You understand new things before anyone else. Tech and digital was made for you! *Role model: Oprah Winfrey.*

PISCES You'll thrive wherever your wisdom is appreciated. Particularly in artistic and creative roles. *Role model: Rihanna.*

PUBLIC SPEAKING SOS

How to prepare for that big presentation

ARIES Match a confident tone to open body language and they'll totally go for it!

TAURUS Perfect preparation will give you the confidence to shine.

GEMINI Deep breaths right before you start will get you calm.

CANCER Imagine you are speaking to just one person in the audience.

LEO Pick a killer outfit and enjoy your moment in the spotlight.

VIRGO Get your cue cards ready to go and visit the venue beforehand.

LIBRA Practise in front of friends and ask for feedback.

SCORPIO Imagine them all naked. Your enigmatic persona will win them over.

SAGITTARIUS Don't leave prep to the last minute – it takes more than just your sparkling personality to win!

CAPRICORN You've run through it about a million times, now don't forget to smile!

AQUARIUS If you're worried about getting the jitters, memorise your speech.

PISCES Grab some CBD oil and do some breathing exercises.

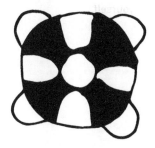

GET EFFICIENT!

Do better, quicker

ARIES Break down long-term projects into manageable stages.

TAURUS Tenacious Taurus is slow to get going. Just dive straight in.

GEMINI You work quickly but sporadically – get more focused!

CANCER Understand who you are supporting in this task to make you feel more motivated.

LEO Use time off as a reward for work completed, and your success rate will soar.

VIRGO Learn to delegate – it's not possible to do it all yourself.

LIBRA Get an accountability partner, work on projects with people.

SCORPIO You are a super-focused sign who has it down!

SAGITTARIUS Talking about it won't make it happen, learn to set measurable goals.

CAPRICORN Learn to ask for help.

AQUARIUS Be honest when you're procrastinating – why are you putting this off?

PISCES Stop making excuses. Set an alarm, set a goal, get to it.

GET SH*T DONE

ARIES, CAPRICORN, LEO, LIBRA

First thing – You are energised and firing on all cylinders. Some of the other signs hate you for it, but make the most of your morning motivation.

GEMINI, TAURUS, CANCER, VIRGO

Mid-morning – You kick into gear around 10 or 11am. Clear your diary and power through before you break for lunch.

SAGITTARIUS, AQUARIUS, PISCES, SCORPIO

Night – You think the best things happen at night anyway, and you really get going in the early hours. Great if that works with your lifestyle, but be careful not to burn out.

ANNOYING COLLEAGUES

Is this you?!

ARIES Always interrupt.

TAURUS Slow on the uptake. Keep up!

GEMINI Click pen and tap foot when thinking.

CANCER Take things way too personally.

LEO Talk too much in meetings.

VIRGO Known for doing everything for your boss.

LIBRA Way too sparkling first thing on a Monday morning.

SCORPIO Moody.

SAGITTARIUS Always late.

CAPRICORN Act like you're the boss, even when you're not.

AQUARIUS Literally no one understands your blue-sky ideas.

PISCES Paperwork goes missing on your chaotic desk.

HOW TO HANDLE YOUR BOSS

ARIES Is a warrior! Don't show weakness and apply a can-do attitude.

TAURUS Is set in their ways. Show them a new way of doing things, but only when they know they can trust you.

GEMINI Is chatty and inconsistent. Expect a last-minute change of plan. Learn to juggle tasks.

CANCER Is caring but bossy. Wants the best for you but can be moody and defensive! Learn to stay steady and calm.

LEO Knows they are the best, commands and demands respect. Praise, flatter and kiss their ass.

VIRGO Likes order and organisation. Follow the rules to get their respect.

LIBRA Wants everyone to be friends. Learn to keep your cool and avoid confrontations that will upset the team dynamic.

SCORPIO Values commitment and concentration. Often a work hard/play hard type - go big or go home.

SAGITTARIUS Is big on vision. Be the employee who makes that vision a reality and rise with them.

CAPRICORN Goes above and beyond what is expected, wants you to do the same.

AQUARIUS Wants to be everyone's friend BUT secretly hates their authority being undermined. Don't forget it.

PISCES May seem chilled, but is obsessive about detail because they fear chaos. Watch carefully to see what makes them tick.

CONSTRUCTIVE CRITICISM

How to deal with negative feedback

CANCER, SCORPIO, TAURUS

Take some time to think it over – try not to instinctively go on the defensive or decide they're just wrong.

ARIES, VIRGO

Stop crying. It's not the end of the world if you're not the best at everything.

LIBRA, CAPRICORN, PISCES

Keep some perspective. You're great at acting on feedback, but don't take everything as gospel.

LEO, AQUARIUS, GEMINI, SAGITTARIUS

Try not to make it your life's mission to prove them wrong. You don't have to organise every team drinks for ever just because someone said you're not a team player.

SICK DAYS

When does your sign call in sick?

 CAPRICORN, SCORPIO, ARIES

Only if near death.

 PISCES, VIRGO, LEO

At the merest hint of a sniffle.

 LIBRA, TAURUS, GEMINI

Whenever they fancy a day off.

 CANCER, AQUARIUS, SAGITTARIUS

When they think they might be contagious.

<u>OUT OF OFFICE</u>

What they put on their ooo

ARIES If it's an emergency please call me. Otherwise, don't.

TAURUS All emails received will be automatically deleted. If it is urgent, email me when I'm back.

GEMINI I will be in the office tomorrow afternoon for 2 hours. My out of office is always on because I'm busy AF. #busy

CANCER Thanks for getting in touch. If it's urgent, please call one of my lovely colleagues. Thanks!

LEO In meetings today, I will get back to you tomorrow (because natch going to be pissed later on). #hospitality

VIRGO I am on annual leave and will be back at my desk at 8.30am on 1 September. I will get back to you as soon as possible.

LIBRA   I am currently out of the office but will still reach out as soon as I receive this :). Have a lovely day.

SCORPIO   I am currently away. *literally no other info*

SAGITTARIUS   I am on holiday in Australia, Indonesia and East Timor! I will be back in a month.

CAPRICORN   Will get back to you ASAP.

AQUARIUS   Thanks for your email. I'll reply when I'm back.

PISCES   *away for two months, did not think to put out of office on*

SIDE HUSTLES

How to make cash from your sign's talents

ARIES Personal trainer. Use that energy to help others reach their goals!

TAURUS Garden designer. Harness your love of the outdoors for cash.

GEMINI Blogger or freelance writer. You've got something to say, so get paid to say it!

CANCER Cake maker. Believe the compliments and turn your skills into a business on the side.

LEO Social media influencer. You're already leading the pack, and companies would love to have you on board.

VIRGO Professional eBayer. You have the dedication and skills to turn trash into cash.

LIBRA Interior decorator. Everyone covets your sense of style – why not turn it into a hustle?

SCORPIO Private detective. Get paid to snoop? Yes please.

SAGITTARIUS Life coach. Who wouldn't love a dose of your positivity and can-do attitude?

CAPRICORN Property developer. Put that big-picture view to good use.

AQUARIUS Start-up founder. Spot the next big thing and make it happen.

PISCES Tarot reader.

YOUR CELESTIAL CV

Three strengths the signs should shout about

ARIES Self-motivated, driven, enterprising.

TAURUS Tenacious, reliable, artistic.

GEMINI Articulate, versatile, people-orientated.

CANCER Thoughtful, caring, hard-working.

LEO Natural leader, confident, authoritative.

VIRGO Detail-orientated, organised, planner.

LIBRA Calm, team leader, imaginative.

SCORPIO Astounding work ethic, knowledgeable, strategic.

SAGITTARIUS Problem-solver, inspires others, confident.

CAPRICORN Ambitious, hard-working, resourceful.

AQUARIUS Innovative, tech savvy, forward thinking.

PISCES Creative, visionary, versatile.

WHAT'S ON YOUR DESK?

You can tell who sits here

ARIES Bike helmet and energy drink.

TAURUS Fruit bowl and pot plants.

GEMINI Hand cream, a nail file, lip balm, body spray.

CANCER Family photos.

LEO Selfies.

VIRGO A huge stack of paperwork and some Post-it notes.

LIBRA Postcards of modern art and a cafetière.

SCORPIO A document shredder.

SAGITTARIUS Crumpled meeting handouts and food wrappers.

CAPRICORN An expensive pen.

AQUARIUS A headset and screen and nothing else.

PISCES All the paperwork everyone else is looking for.

THE TEA ROUND

Whose turn is it to put the kettle on?

ARIES Makes weak tea, as they're too impatient.

TAURUS Makes their own, as they are so fussy.

GEMINI Still chatting in the kitchen 20 minutes after offering everyone tea.

CANCER Will only drink from their special mug.

LEO Only does the tea round once a week, but always brings cake.

VIRGO Doesn't drink tea, but still always stuck doing the tea round.

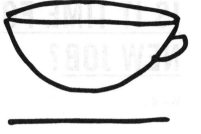

LIBRA Is in an exclusive tea round with one special 'tea friend'.

SCORPIO Makes their own, refuses to get involved.

SAGITTARIUS Drinks chai blend in a stupidly large mug.

CAPRICORN Doesn't believe in the tea round and does not wish to be interrupted.

AQUARIUS What tea round?

PISCES All the missing mugs are eventually found, dirty, buried on Pisces' desk.

IS IT TIME FOR A NEW JOB?

Yes if . . .

ARIES You don't have the chance to use your initiative.

TAURUS There's a lack of job security or your creative talents are underused.

GEMINI Your excellent admin skills get you stuck in a stifling support role.

CANCER The company has grown too much and feels impersonal.

LEO A new manager is employed above you and is driving you mad.

VIRGO Your anxiety is through the roof – go for a fresh start with clear boundaries.

LIBRA There's not enough opportunity to meet and charm people.

SCORPIO Your hard work is being unappreciated.

SAGITTARIUS Boredom is making you slapdash.

CAPRICORN You realise you're being underpaid.

AQUARIUS It feels like your company is behind the curve.

PISCES Your creative genius is being overlooked.

YOU'RE FIRED!

Why the signs get the sack

ARIES They threw a tantrum and told the boss to shove it.

TAURUS They flatly refused to do the 5,453rd inane task.

GEMINI For spreading rumours.

CANCER They finally lost their sh*t and let rip with everything they've been bottling up for years.

LEO For going rogue and making terrible decisions.

VIRGO Not technically sacked, just told to take a sabbatical for their nerves.

LIBRA For having a prohibited love affair with their boss.

SCORPIO They were grooming clients to poach for their own business.

SAGITTARIUS Forgot to come back from holiday.

CAPRICORN Managed out for going over their boss's head.

AQUARIUS They told a rude client to f*ck off.

PISCES For getting their dealer to stop by the office when smashed at a work party.

MOON & RISING SIGNS

WHAT IS MY MOON SIGN?

The exact position of everything in the night sky at the moment you were born has an impact on who you are and how you feel about stuff. The moon only stays around in each sign for two days at a time as it moves across the sky, but it is intimately connected to how you really feel, deep down. In particular, the moon represents our loving nature and how we nurture ourselves. It can compound elements of your star sign or add hidden, conflicting depths. You can look up your moon sign on www.francescaoddie.com – you'll need to know your birth time. Your moon sign has a big influence on who you are in your relationships, so you might want to think about whether the description below feels true for you, and read the dating section with your moon hat on ...

ARIES Can be hard to live with as they react explosively to their emotions. Security is important to Aries. They are incapable of sitting still and their idea of recuperation is to do stuff.

TAURUS Calm, contented and happy when they feel comfortable, fed and cosy. Taurus's natural inner state is pretty chilled, and other signs whose emotions are more unstable find them soothing to be around.

GEMINI Geminis want to talk, text and generally communicate, as it makes them feel loved and connected. The Gemini moon needs to know all about loved ones – what they ate, how they slept, where they've been ...

CANCER Kind Cancer moon will feed, hug and look after you. However, sometimes they become overwhelmed by their own emotions, come across as really moody and need to retreat from the world.

LEO Leos have a strong inner sense of self-worth that gets them through tough situations, even if everyone else thinks they can be a bit of a princess! Those with a Leo moon are independent-minded and do what they want.

VIRGO The fusspot moon! Virgos have a strong need to control their environment. They can come across as quite critical, but it all comes from a place of love, and wanting to help.

LIBRA Libras have a real need to feel like everything is in balance. Conflict and uncertainty is challenging for a Libra moon. Conversations with family and friends reassure them and make them feel loved.

SCORPIO Scorpios want to love intensely and be loved, though they often instinctively repress what they feel because it is so strong. Scorpio moons can read between the lines and are often natural psychologists.

SAGITTARIUS The free spirit. Those with a Sagittarius moon are most at peace when they are free to roam. They love to learn new things, try foreign cuisine and generally explore the world.

CAPRICORN Very cautious with their emotions, Capricorns are responsible when dealing with the emotions of others. Measurable achievement is central to their sense of self-worth.

AQUARIUS Aquarians can come across as emotionally detached, though they are usually very friendly. The Aquarius moon is the least comfortable with normal emotional functions and needs lots of space.

PISCES Nurturing and caring, although Pisces' extreme empathy means they can get emotionally burnt out and need alone time to recharge. The Pisces moon is very intuitive, to the point where they can seem psychic.

WHAT IS MY RISING SIGN?

The zodiac sign that was emerging over the eastern horizon at your time of birth, known as your rising sign, or ascendant, is an important one. Your rising sign influences the way people perceive you, as well as the lens through which you see the world. It's also the mask you wear in new situations. If you don't know it then you can look it up on www.francescaoddie. com – you do need to know your time of birth to the nearest minute. Once you've figured it out, ask your friends if this sounds like you . . .

ARIES Comes across as decisive, direct, impulsive. Those with Aries rising are often athletic-looking and have strong eyebrows!

TAURUS Projects a steady, calm, unassuming persona. They are also pretty hot – loads of models have Taurus rising.

GEMINI Always asking questions. This rising sign can bring an air of restlessness and impatience. They are generally very clever and always observing the world around them.

CANCER Often comes across as shy, but people always pick up on their kindness and consideration to others. They tend to have girl/guy next door-style good looks.

LEO Easy to spot as they're all about bright colours, with perhaps bleached hair or a penchant for animal print. Can be heard loudly giving compliments to everyone!

VIRGO Comes across as quiet and unassuming. Those with Virgo rising often wear specs. Check their bag for a diary or planner.

LIBRA Always groomed to perfection with the perfect shoes for their outfit. Those with Libra rising are very hospitable and remember everyone's names.

SCORPIO Have penetrating eyes that look right into you! Though they often come across as secretive, and it can be hard to get to know them.

SAGITTARIUS A loud, clumsy, larger-than-life character. Those with Sag rising crash through life unafraid to tell you what you think!

CAPRICORN Comes across as mature, sensible and responsible, even when the rest of their chart is more fun and wild. Look out for their heavy eyebrows, good bone structure and strong teeth.

AQUARIUS This rising sign projects an unconventional vibe. They may go for an androgynous look, and can come across as aloof and cool.

PISCES Usually seen as gentle, slightly confused dreamers, who are lacking boundaries. They tend to have big kind eyes in a watery colour.

10 9 8 7 6 5 4 3 2 1

Published in 2019 by Ebury Press an imprint of Ebury Publishing,

20 Vauxhall Bridge Road,
London SW1V 2SA

Ebury Press is part of the Penguin Random House group of companies
whose addresses can be found at global.penguinrandomhouse.com

Penguin
Random House
UK

Liz Marvin and Francesca Oddie have asserted their right to be identified
as the authors of this Work in accordance with the Copyright, Designs and
Patents Act 1988

First published by Pop Press in 2019
www.penguin.co.uk

A CIP catalogue record for this book is available from the British Library

ISBN 978 1 529 10522 3

Designed and illustrated by Lindsay Kelly
Printed and bound in Great Britain by Clays Ltd, Elcograf S.p.A.

MIX
Paper from
responsible sources
FSC® C018179

Penguin Random House is committed to a
sustainable future for our business, our
readers and our planet. This book is made
from Forest Stewardship® certified paper.

ABOUT THE AUTHORS

Francesca Oddie is a straight-talking astrologer and Sagittarius. She is on a quest to show that astrology is a blend of intuition and science, but that doesn't mean you can't have fun with it too!

www.francescaoddie.com

Liz Marvin is a humour and gift book writer and a cynical Pisces. Over the course of writing this book, she has been delighted to find out that her love of wine is totally her star sign's fault.